D1631918

**EMPOWERING QUOTES FOR
GIRLS WHO ARE WILD & FREE**

you grow girl

summersdale

YOU GROW GIRL

An Hachette UK Company
www.hachette.co.uk

Summersdale Publishers Ltd
Part of Octopus Publishing Group Limited
Carmelite House
50 Victoria Embankment
LONDON
EC4Y 0DZ
UK

www.summersdale.com

Printed and bound in China

ISBN: 978-1-78783-677-8

Substantial discounts on bulk quantities of Summersdale books are available to corporations, professional associations and other organizations. For details contact general enquiries: telephone: +44 (0) 1243 771107 or email: enquiries@summersdale.com.

TO....................................

FROM...............................

Ride the energy of your own unique spirit.

GABRIELLE ROTH

YOU ARE MORE
POWERFUL
THAN YOU
KNOW.

MELISSA ETHERIDGE

I love myself when
I am laughing...
and then again when
I am looking mean
and impressive.

ZORA NEALE HURSTON

Bloom

WHERE YOU ARE

planted

Forever is composed of Nows.

EMILY DICKINSON

I DON'T
GET BITTER,
I JUST GET
BETTER.

Rihanna

flower
yourself
with praise

I'd rather have
roses on my table
than diamonds
on my neck.

EMMA GOLDMAN

The most effective way to do it is to do it.

Amelia Earhart

SOMETIMES
YOU GOTTA
BE A BEAUTY
AND A BEAST.

Nicki Minaj

IF YOU HELP
SOMEONE
ELSE SUCCEED,
YOU TOO
SHALL SUCCEED.

 GINA RODRIGUEZ

GIRL, YOU
GOT THIS

I'm not bossy.
I'm the boss.

BEYONCÉ

Cultivate the acquaintance of Mother Nature. She may enrich you.

MINNA ANTRIM

Let your
true self
unfurl

THE EXCITEMENT OF
DREAMS COMING
TRUE IS BEYOND
THE DESCRIPTION
OF WORDS.

LAILAH GIFTY AKITA

I FINALLY GOT
MY ANSWER TO
THAT QUESTION:
WHO DO YOU
THINK YOU ARE?
I AM WHOEVER
I SAY I AM.

 AMERICA FERRERA

If you rest,
you rust.

HELEN HAYES

WE MUST
BELIEVE WE
ARE GIFTED FOR
SOMETHING AND
THAT THIS THING,
AT WHATEVER
COST, MUST BE
ATTAINED.

———

 MARIE CURIE

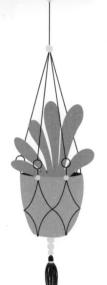

YOU HAVE
TO HAVE
CONFIDENCE IN
YOUR ABILITY,
AND THEN
BE TOUGH
ENOUGH
TO FOLLOW
THROUGH.

Rosalynn Carter

I am no longer
accepting the things
I cannot change. I am
changing the things
I cannot accept.

ANGELA DAVIS

ACTUALLY,

I can

There are multiple sides to all of us. Who we are — and who we might be if we follow our dreams.

MILEY CYRUS

WE HAVE TO
DARE TO BE
OURSELVES,
HOWEVER
FRIGHTENING
OR STRANGE
THAT SELF MAY
PROVE TO BE.

———

 MAY SARTON

All of us are put in
boxes... some people
have the courage
to break free.

Geena Rocero

BE YOURSELF. NO ONE ELSE CAN.

 HELENA BONHAM CARTER

DON'T BE
AFRAID TO
SPEAK UP
FOR YOURSELF.
KEEP FIGHTING
FOR YOUR
DREAMS!

Gabby Douglas

I'd rather regret
the things I've
done than regret
the things I
haven't done.

LUCILLE BALL

Get your
grow on

I want to encourage
women to embrace
their own uniqueness.
Because just like a rose
is beautiful, so is a
sunflower, so is a peony.

MIRANDA KERR

IF YOU
DON'T RISK
ANYTHING,
YOU RISK
EVEN MORE.

ERICA JONG

I never
underestimated
myself. And I never
saw anything wrong
with ambition.

ANGELA MERKEL

Empowered

WOMEN EMPOWER

women

THE BEST
PROTECTION
ANY WOMAN
CAN HAVE IS
COURAGE.

Elizabeth Cady Stanton

Ain't I a woman?

SOJOURNER TRUTH

Girl
flower
power

If they don't give you
a seat at the table, bring
a folding chair.

Shirley Chisholm

SOMETIMES THE
SMALLEST STEP
IN THE RIGHT
DIRECTION ENDS
UP BEING THE
BIGGEST STEP
OF YOUR LIFE.

 EMMA STONE

Never grow
a wishbone,
daughter, where
your backbone
ought to be.

CLEMENTINE PADDLEFORD

YOUNG GIRLS ARE
TOLD THAT THEY HAVE
TO BE THIS KIND
OF PRINCESS – IF I
WAS GOING TO BE A
PRINCESS, I'D BE A
WARRIOR PRINCESS.

EMMA WATSON

GIRLS
CAN

I learned to make my mind large, as the universe is large, so that there is room for paradoxes.

MAXINE HONG KINGSTON

A DAME
THAT KNOWS
THE ROPES
ISN'T LIKELY TO
GET TIED UP.

Mae West

BE A GIRL
WITH A MIND,
A WOMAN
WITH ATTITUDE
AND A LADY
WITH CLASS

Above all,
be the heroine
of your life.

NORA EPHRON

There is no chance,
no destiny, no fate,
that can circumvent
or hinder or control
the firm resolve of a
determined soul.

ELLA WHEELER WILCOX

I'm not intimidated
by how people
perceive me.

Dolly Parton

I've never
been interested
in being invisible
and erased.

LAVERNE COX

IF ONE GIRL
WITH COURAGE
IS A REVOLUTION,
IMAGINE WHAT
FEATS WE CAN
ACHIEVE TOGETHER.

QUEEN RANIA OF JORDAN

lift each
other up

My coach said
I ran like a girl;
I said if he ran
a little faster,
he could too.

MIA HAMM

WOMEN ARE
POWERFUL AND
DANGEROUS.

Audre Lorde

THE GRASS IS

greener

WHERE YOU

water it

Love your flaws.
Own your quirks.
And know that you
are just as perfect
as anyone else,
exactly as you are.

ARIANA GRANDE

You are your
best thing.

TONI MORRISON

A strong woman
looks a challenge
dead in the eye and
gives it a wink.

Gina Carey

THOSE WHO
DWELL AMONG
THE BEAUTIES
AND MYSTERIES
OF THE EARTH
ARE NEVER
ALONE OR
WEARY OF LIFE.

 RACHEL CARSON

DON'T WAIT
FOR SOMEONE
TO BRING YOU
FLOWERS -
PLANT YOUR
OWN

There is no limit
to what we,
as women, can
accomplish.

MICHELLE OBAMA

I'VE BEEN
THROUGH IT
ALL, BABY.
I'M MOTHER
COURAGE.

ELIZABETH TAYLOR

Be the best version of yourself

I identify as
what I am.

Andreja Pejić

I AM NOT A
HAS-BEEN.
I AM A
WILL BE.

Lauren Bacall

Grow through

WHAT YOU GO

go through

I'm not interested in money. I just want to be wonderful.

MARILYN MONROE

Living out loud is
living a life that's
bigger than yourself.
You leave something
on this earth that's
bigger than yourself.

VIOLA DAVIS

In a wild world, stay true to you

If you think taking care
of yourself is selfish,
change your mind.

Ann Richards

If you can believe
in something great,
then you can achieve
something great.

KATY PERRY

ALL GOOD
THINGS ARE
WILD AND
FREE

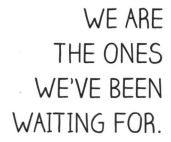

WE ARE
THE ONES
WE'VE BEEN
WAITING FOR.

JUNE JORDAN

Run to the fire;
don't hide from it.

MEG WHITMAN

DON'T SETTLE
FOR AVERAGE.
BRING YOUR
BEST TO THE
MOMENT.

Angela Bassett

IF YOU DON'T
SEE A CLEAR
PATH FOR WHAT
YOU WANT,
SOMETIMES YOU
HAVE TO MAKE
IT YOURSELF.

MINDY KALING

Your life belongs to
you and you alone.

CHIMAMANDA NGOZI ADICHIE

MAKE IT

happen

Speaking your truth
is the most powerful
tool we all have.

Oprah Winfrey

Let us pick up our books and our pens. They are the most powerful weapons.

MALALA YOUSAFZAI

The most common way
people give up their
power is by thinking
they don't have any.

ALICE WALKER

I AM A FULL
WOMAN AND
I'M STRONG, AND
I'M POWERFUL,
AND I'M
BEAUTIFUL AT
THE SAME TIME.

 SERENA WILLIAMS

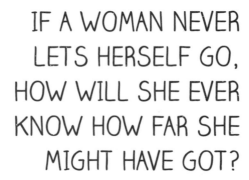

IF A WOMAN NEVER
LETS HERSELF GO,
HOW WILL SHE EVER
KNOW HOW FAR SHE
MIGHT HAVE GOT?

GERMAINE GREER

If you prioritize yourself, you are going to save yourself.

GABRIELLE UNION

yes girl,
yes!

THE MOST
BEAUTIFUL
WOMAN IN
THE WORLD IS
THE ONE WHO
PROTECTS AND
SUPPORTS
OTHER WOMEN.

 SANDRA BULLOCK

Different is good. When someone tells you that you are different, smile and hold your head up and be proud.

ANGELINA JOLIE

ADVENTURE IS
WORTHWHILE
IN ITSELF.

Amelia Earhart

I think the best role models for women are people who are fruitfully and confidently themselves.

MERYL STREEP

Respect

YOUR

roots

Don't ever
forget your worth...
you are enough.

Meghan, Duchess of Sussex

When a woman rises up in glory, her energy is magnetic and her sense of possibility contagious.

MARIANNE WILLIAMSON

Oh,
how she
blossoms

ONCE YOU
FIGURE OUT WHO
YOU ARE AND
WHAT YOU LOVE
ABOUT YOURSELF,
I THINK IT ALL
KIND OF FALLS
INTO PLACE.

 JENNIFER ANISTON

I AM HERE.
I AM WHOLE.
I AM ABLE.

ALEXANDRA ELLE

We are each made differently, so find whatever flaw or imperfection you have and start embracing it because it's part of you.

DEMI LOVATO

I have standards
I don't plan
on lowering
for anybody –
including myself.

ZENDAYA

I WILL
GROW

EVERY
WOMAN
IS A QUEEN,
AND WE
ALL HAVE
DIFFERENT
THINGS TO
OFFER.

Queen Latifah

To succeed in life,
you need three things:
a wishbone, a backbone
and a funny bone.

REBA McENTIRE

you can
never cut
me down

Don't let anyone
steal ya joy!

Missy Elliott

Invest in your brain, invest in your talents.

RASHIDA JONES

MY MOTTO IS:
"I'M ALIVE, SO
THAT MEANS I CAN
DO ANYTHING."

VENUS WILLIAMS

'TIS WOMAN'S
STRONGEST
VINDICATION
FOR SPEAKING
THAT THE WORLD
NEEDS TO HEAR
HER VOICE.

 ANNA J. COOPER

Happiness

STEMS FROM

self-love

I live my life because I dare.

GABOUREY SIDIBE

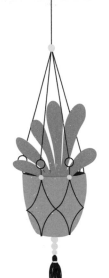

I LOVE MY
REJECTION
SLIPS. THEY
SHOW ME
I TRY.

Sylvia Plath

I will
flourish

Take up the battle.
Take it up. It's yours.
This is your life.
This is your world.

MAYA ANGELOU

Learning what
makes you feel good
in your own skin is like
reclaiming something
that you weren't
even aware had been
taken from you.

FRANCES RYAN

Embrace what makes
you unique, even
if it makes others
uncomfortable.

Janelle Monáe

You need to find
the power within to
make things happen
for yourself. When
you realize this, you
are unstoppable.

CHRISTINA AGUILERA

I WILL NOT ASK
THAT YOU NOR
YOU APPROVE.
THE WILD THYME
IS ITSELF NOR
ASKS CONSENT
OF ROSE
NOR REED.

MURIEL STRODE

THE QUESTION ISN'T
WHO IS GOING TO
LET ME; IT'S WHO IS
GOING TO STOP ME?

AYN RAND

Exceed YOUR expectations

Women speaking up
for themselves and for
those around them is the
strongest force we have
to change the world.

MELINDA GATES

No matter where
you are from, your
dreams are valid.

LUPITA NYONG'O

I THINK WOMEN
PLAY A MAJOR
PART IN OPENING
THE DOORS
FOR BETTER
UNDERSTANDING
AROUND THE
WORLD.

 NINA SIMONE

ALL THE MARKS
ON THE WORLD
MEAN NOTHING
COMPARED TO
THE MARKS
YOU'RE ABOUT
TO MAKE.

Amber Tamblyn

I just don't believe in perfection. But I do believe in saying, "This is who I am and look at me not being perfect!"

KATE WINSLET

Better to live
one year as a tiger,
than a hundred
as a sheep.

MADONNA

Naturally badass

Who knows what women can be when they are finally free to become themselves?

BETTY FRIEDAN

It's not your
job to like me,
it's mine.

Byron Katie

HOW IMPORTANT
IT IS FOR US
TO RECOGNIZE
AND CELEBRATE
OUR HEROES
AND SHE-ROES!

MAYA ANGELOU

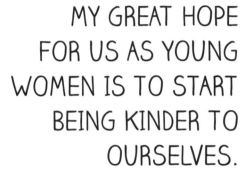

MY GREAT HOPE
FOR US AS YOUNG
WOMEN IS TO START
BEING KINDER TO
OURSELVES.

EMMA STONE

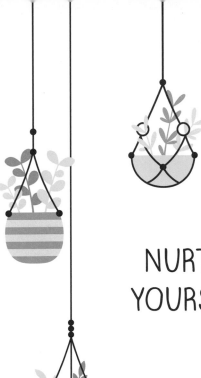

NURTURE
YOURSELF

OTHER WOMEN
WHO ARE KILLING
IT SHOULD
MOTIVATE YOU,
THRILL YOU,
CHALLENGE YOU,
AND INSPIRE YOU.

 TAYLOR SWIFT

Change your life today. Don't gamble on the future, act now, without delay.

SIMONE DE BEAUVOIR

weed out
negativity

There have been so many people who have said to me, "You can't do that," but I've had an innate belief that they were wrong. Be unwavering and relentless in your approach.

HALLE BERRY

YOU ARE
ALLOWED TO BE
RADICAL AND
HAVE STRONG
THOUGHTS
THAT OTHERS
MIGHT NOT
AGREE WITH.

Alicia Keys

Womanhood is
everything that's
inside of you.

VIOLA DAVIS

Women are not inherently
passive or peaceful.
We're not inherently
anything but human.

Robin Morgan

YOU'RE A

limited

edition

Stay afraid, but
do it anyway.
What's important
is the action.

CARRIE FISHER

To girls and women
everywhere, I issue
a simple invitation.
My sisters, my
daughters, my friends:
find your voice.

ELLEN JOHNSON SIRLEAF

Root for
yourself!

I BELIEVE AMBITION
IS NOT A DIRTY WORD.
IT'S JUST BELIEVING
IN YOURSELF AND
YOUR ABILITIES.

REESE WITHERSPOON

I'M TOUGH,
I'M AMBITIOUS,
AND I KNOW
EXACTLY WHAT
I WANT. IF THAT
MAKES ME A
BITCH, OKAY.

 MADONNA

It's never too late to take a leap of faith and see what will happen – and to be brave in life.

JANE FONDA

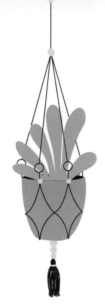

I'D RATHER
REGRET THE
RISKS THAT
DIDN'T WORK
OUT THAN THE
CHANCES I
DIDN'T TAKE
AT ALL.

Simone Biles

BELIEVE
IN YOUR
GOODNESS

Act the way you want to feel.

GRETCHEN RUBIN

There's no better
make-up than
self-confidence.

Shakira

Fight like a girl

No one can make you feel inferior without your consent.

ELEANOR ROOSEVELT

JUST ENJOY EVERY MOMENT — DON'T STRESS. JUST BE YOURSELF.

MABEL

First love is self-love.

BELL HOOKS

IN SEARCH OF
MY MOTHER'S
GARDEN,
I FOUND
MY OWN.

 ALICE WALKER

YOU GROW,
GIRL!

If you're interested in finding out more about our books, find us on Facebook at **Summersdale Publishers** and follow us on Twitter at **@Summersdale**.

www.summersdale.com

Image credits